WORKBOOK

ENSINO FUNDAMENTAL
ANOS INICIAIS

RENATO MENDES CURTO JÚNIOR
ANNA CAROLINA GUIMARÃES
CIBELE MENDES

CONTENTS

UNIT

1 IT'S TIME FOR GOOD THINGS!

1 Circle all the items we can find in a classroom.

Ilustrações: Maira Nakazaki

2 Now, write the names of all the objects you circled.

____

____

3 Complete the sentences with the correct name of the object and paint the pictures according to their description.

a) This is a yellow ________________.

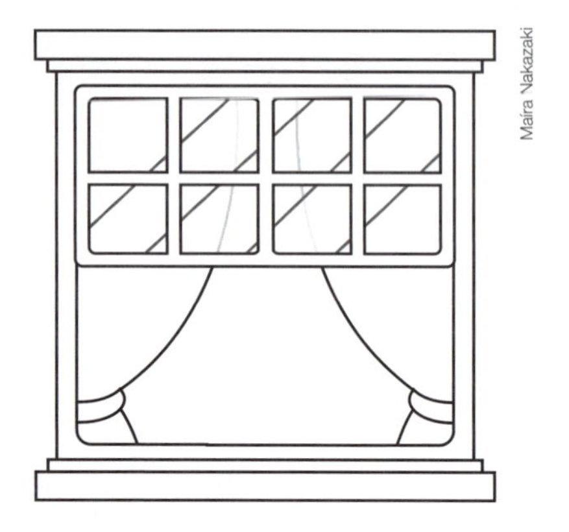

d) This is a green ________________ and this is a red ________________.

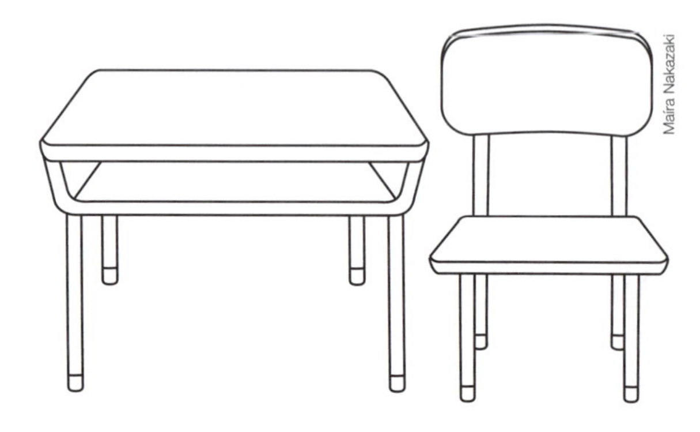

b) This is a brown and purple ________________.

e) This is an orange ________________.

c) This is a blue ________________.

f) This is a grey ________________.

4 Make a list of the furniture and objects you can see in your classroom.

- ______________________________.
- ______________________________.
- ______________________________.
- ______________________________.
- ______________________________.
- ______________________________.
- ______________________________.
- ______________________________.
- ______________________________.
- ______________________________.
- ______________________________.

5 Now imagine you took a picture of your classroom from the ceiling, using a drone. On a sheet of paper, draw what you can see in the picture, this means, draw a floor plan of your classroom.
Example of a classroom floor plan.

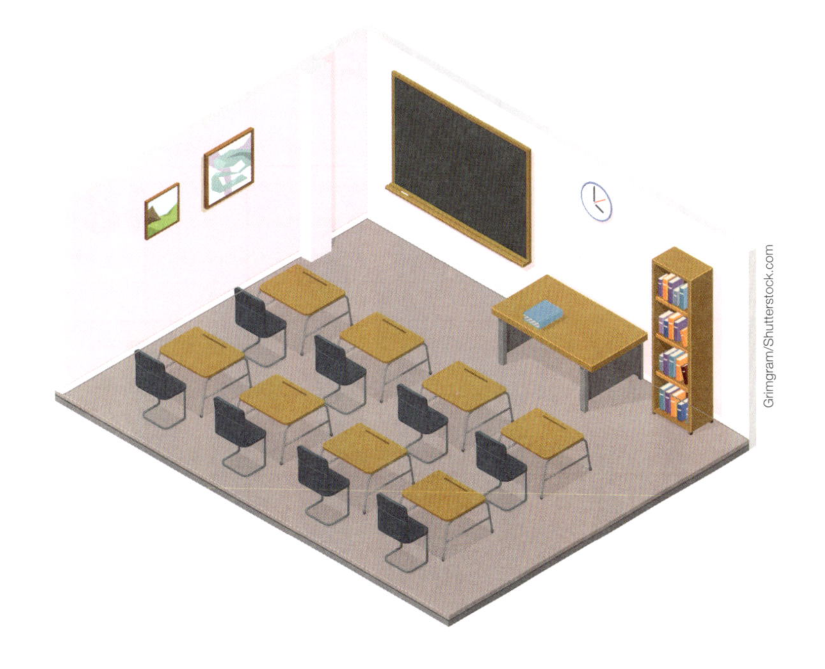
Grimgram/Shutterstock.com

UNIT

2 GAMES AND FUN

1 Complete the sequence with the missing numbers.

____ twenty	21 ____	____ twenty-two	23 ____	24 ____
25 ____	26 ____	27 ____	____ twenty-eight	29 ____
30 ____	____ thirty-one	32 ____	33 ____	____ thirty-four
35 ____	36 ____	____ thirty-seven	38 ____	39 ____
____ forty	41 ____	42 ____	____ forty-three	44 ____
45 ____	____ forty-six	47 ____	48 ____	____ forty-nine
50 ____	51 ____	____ fifty-two	53 ____	____ fifty-four
____ fifty-five	56 ____	____ fifty-seven	58 ____	____ fifty-nine

2 Write the numbers in the crossword puzzle.

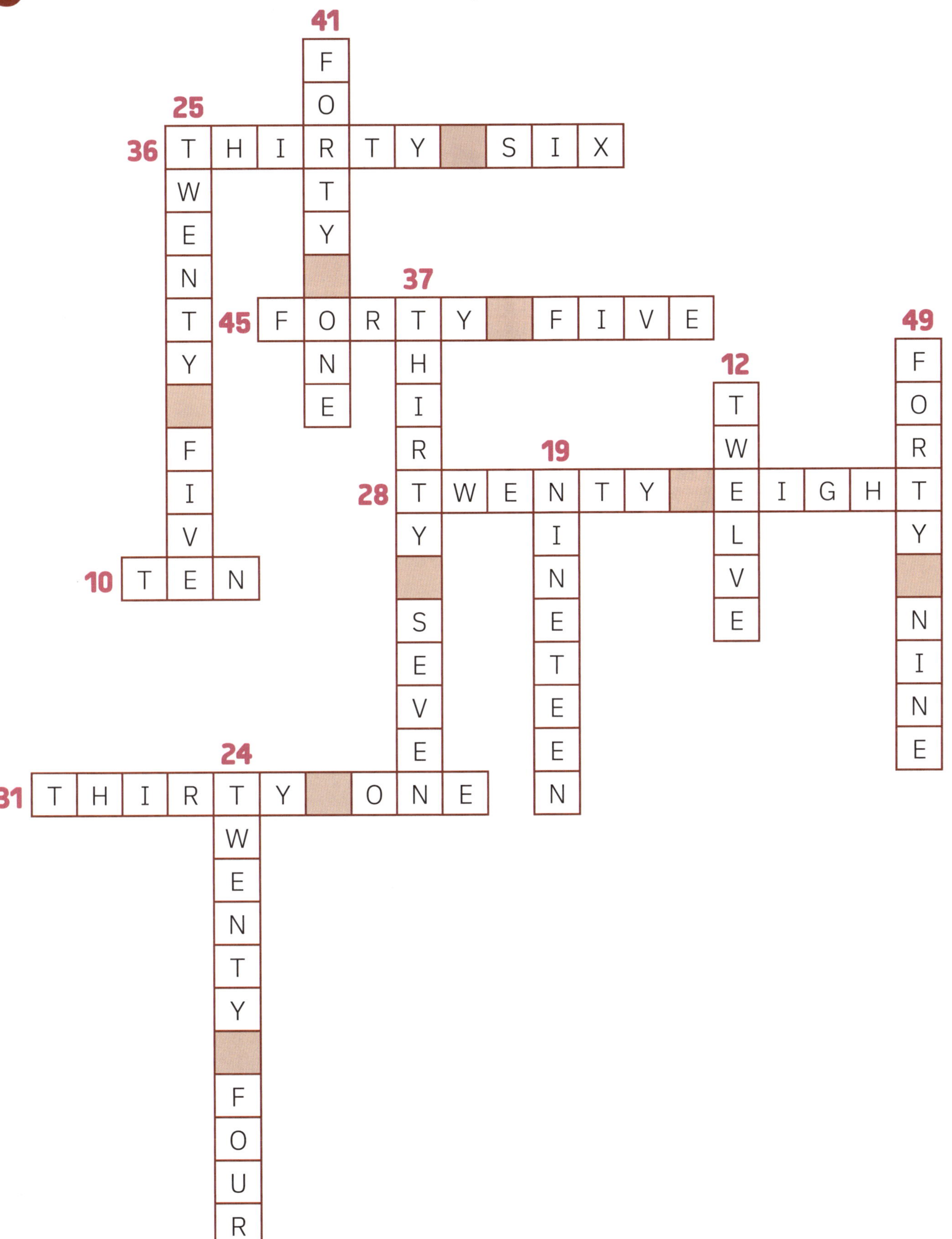

3 Let's play "Simon says"! Follow your teacher's instructions.

Simon says...

- Open your mouth wide.
- Clap your hands.
- Blow kisses.
- Pick up your notebook.
- Make a funny face.
- Wave hello.

UNIT

3 THE FARM

1 What is its name?

a)

Marcos de Mello

____

b)

Marcos de Mello

____

c)

Marcos de Mello

____

d)

Marcos de Mello

____

e)

Marcos de Mello

____

f)

Marcos de Mello

____

g)

Spreadthesign/shutterstock.com

____

h)

Luiz Lentini

____

2 Organize the animals into the correct categories.

Horse • Chicken • Bird • Elephant
Cow • Cat • Lion • Monkey

Pet	Farm	Zoo

3 What animal is it?

a)

Vlad Klok/Shutterstock.com

____

c)

Vlad Klok/Shutterstock.com

____

b)

Vlad Klok/Shutterstock.com

____

d)

Vlad Klok/Shutterstock.com

____

4 What is the correct form of the verb **to like** for each sentence?

a) I ______________ cats and lions.

b) He ______________ birds and horses.

c) I ______________ cows and chickens.

d) She ______________ elephants and giraffes.

5 Have you ever been to a farm during a vacation? Which of these animals did you see there? Using the following words from the list, complete the crossword puzzle.

- Chicken
- Cow
- Duck
- Horse
- Pig
- Rabbit
- Sheep
- Donkey

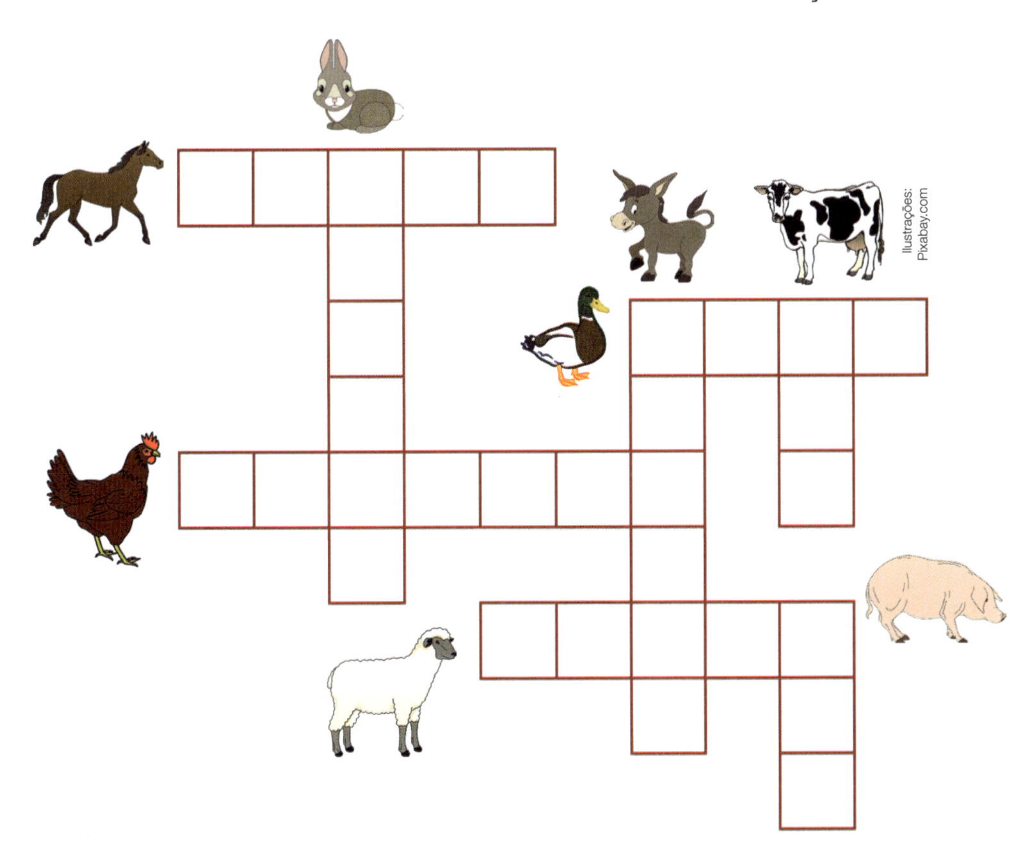

UNIT

OUR WINTER VACATION

1 What season is it? Write the correct name.

a) 

____

c) 

Ilustrações: Luiz Lentini

____

b) 

____

d) 

____

2 Circle all the activities we do in the winter.

To sleep in	To drink a hot beverage
To eat ice cream	To wear light clothes
To swim	To make a snowman
To wear warm clothes	To enjoy the sun

3 Choose the correct option.

a)

☐ young ☐ old

b)

☐ young ☐ old

c)

☐ hot ☐ cold

d)

☐ hot ☐ cold

e)

☐ fast ☐ slow

f)

☐ fast ☐ slow

g)

☐ big ☐ small

h)

☐ big ☐ small

i)

☐ happy ☐ sad

j)

☐ happy ☐ sad

Maira Nakazaki
Carolita Sartório
Carolita Sartório
Maira Nakazaki
Maira Nakazaki
Carolita Sartório
Carolita Sartório
Maira Nakazaki
Carolita Sartório
Maira Nakazaki

4 Match the adjectives to their opposites.

Big	Tall
Happy	Old
New	Empty
Clean	Slow
Full	Small
Beautiful	Ugly
Short	Sad
Cold	Dirty
Fast	Hot

5 Now, listen to your teacher and circle the correct picture.

6 It is winter! Find these hidden words: CHOCOLATE, CLOTHES, SNOW, SNOWMAN. They are in the vertical and horizontal positions.

V	S	H	L	A	U	Y	X	E	M	U	I
D	N	Q	T	O	K	K	D	S	F	L	W
P	O	M	S	N	O	W	M	A	N	E	Z
Z	W	W	F	M	D	F	M	S	N	O	G
S	V	S	V	G	D	A	Q	Z	C	Z	T
C	H	O	C	O	L	A	T	E	D	B	P
T	W	B	M	D	X	O	P	H	T	H	I
F	O	H	C	C	L	O	T	H	E	S	X

7 Now follow the instructions to paint the snowman's winter clothes.

- The hat is blue and green.
- The scarf is purple and orange.
- The gloves are blue.

Евгения/Pixabay.com

UNIT

HEALTHY FOOD

1 Color the fruits according to the colors indicated in the sentences.

- A yellow banana.
- A red apple.
- A green pear.
- An orange peach.
- A yellow and black papaya.
- A red and black strawberry.

Luiz Lentini

Eduardo Belmiro

Luiz Lentini

Eduardo Belmiro

nikiteev_konstantin/Shutterstock.com

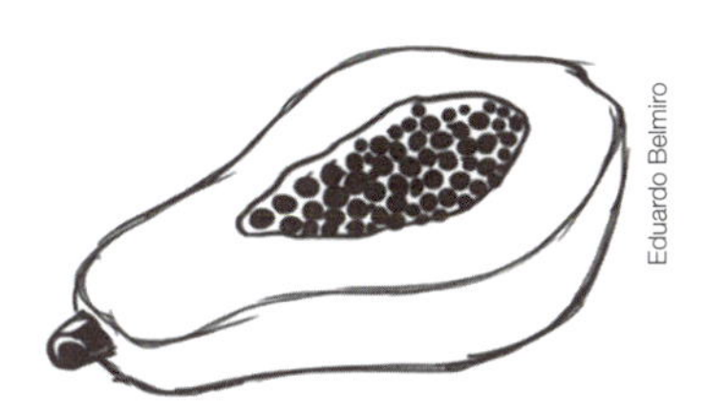

Eduardo Belmiro

2 Unscramble the letters and find the foods' names.

a) adnscihw:

____

b) astke:

____

c) rFcneh sirfe:

____

d) nagoer uceji:

____

e) aosd:

____

f) raewt:

____

3 Complete the blank spaces with the modal verb **would** or **would like**.

Waitress: What ______________________________ you like to order?

Peter: I ______________________________ a lasagna and a pineapple juice, please.

Lucia: I ______________________________ a hamburger and French fries, please.

4 What is their favorite meal? Read and draw.

a) My favorite meal is pasta, beef and orange juice.

b) My favorite meal is salad, rice, beans and fish.

5 Match the image and the name of the vegetables and fruits to the colors.

Ciker-Free-Vector-Images/Pixabay.com

Lettuce

Yellow

Ciker-Free-Vector-Images/Pixabay.com

Banana

Green

OpenClipart-Vectors/Pixabay.com

Apple

Orange

Mostafa Elturkey/Pixabay.com

Carrot

Red

6 Color the food according to the titles.

Red strawberry

donpiano/Pixabay.com

Green beans

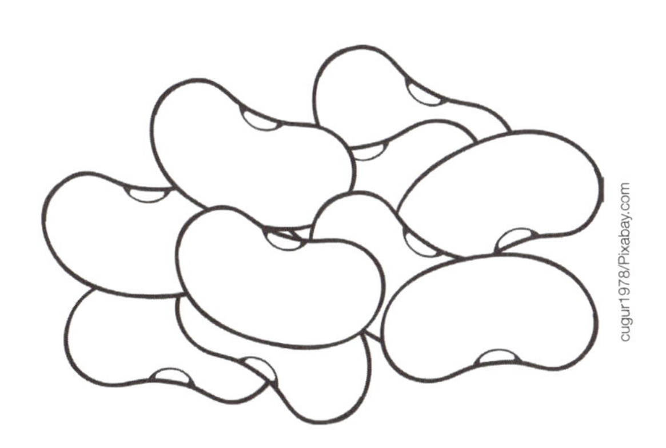

cugur1978/Pixabay.com

Yellow cheese

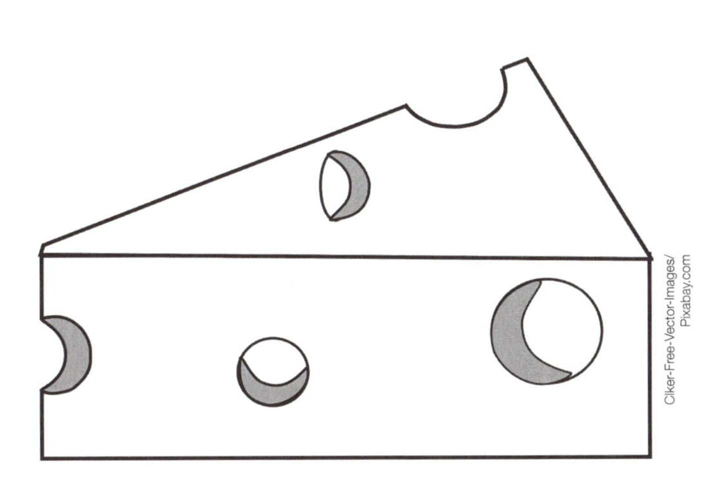

Clker-Free-Vector-Images/Pixabay.com

Orange pumpkin

Clker-Free-Vector-Images/Pixabay.com

7 Write questions with **would you like**. Follow the example below.

a)

Vasilyeva Larisa/Shutterstock.com

— **Would you like** to eat a hamburger?

— No, thanks! I'm not hungry.

b)

pixelliebe/Shutterstock.com

— ______________________ soccer?

— Yes, I love playing soccer!

c)

Mary Long/Shutterstock.com

— ______________________?

— Sure! I am very tired and I need to sleep!

d)

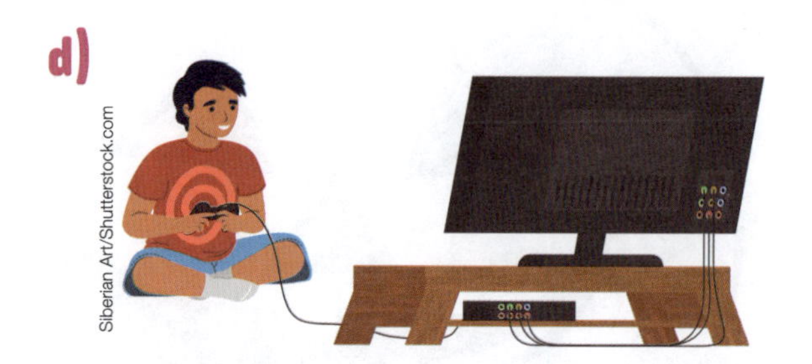

Siberian Art/Shutterstock.com

— ______________________?

— Oh, sure! I love video games!

8 Complete the mind map with these words: ORANGE, LETTUCE, SPINACH, FISH, WATERMELON, COOKIES, CARROTS, APPLES, CAKE, ICE CREAM, SODA, POTATOES, JUICE, GRAPES, MILK, BROCCOLI, TEA, WATER, PAPAYA. Put them in the right category.

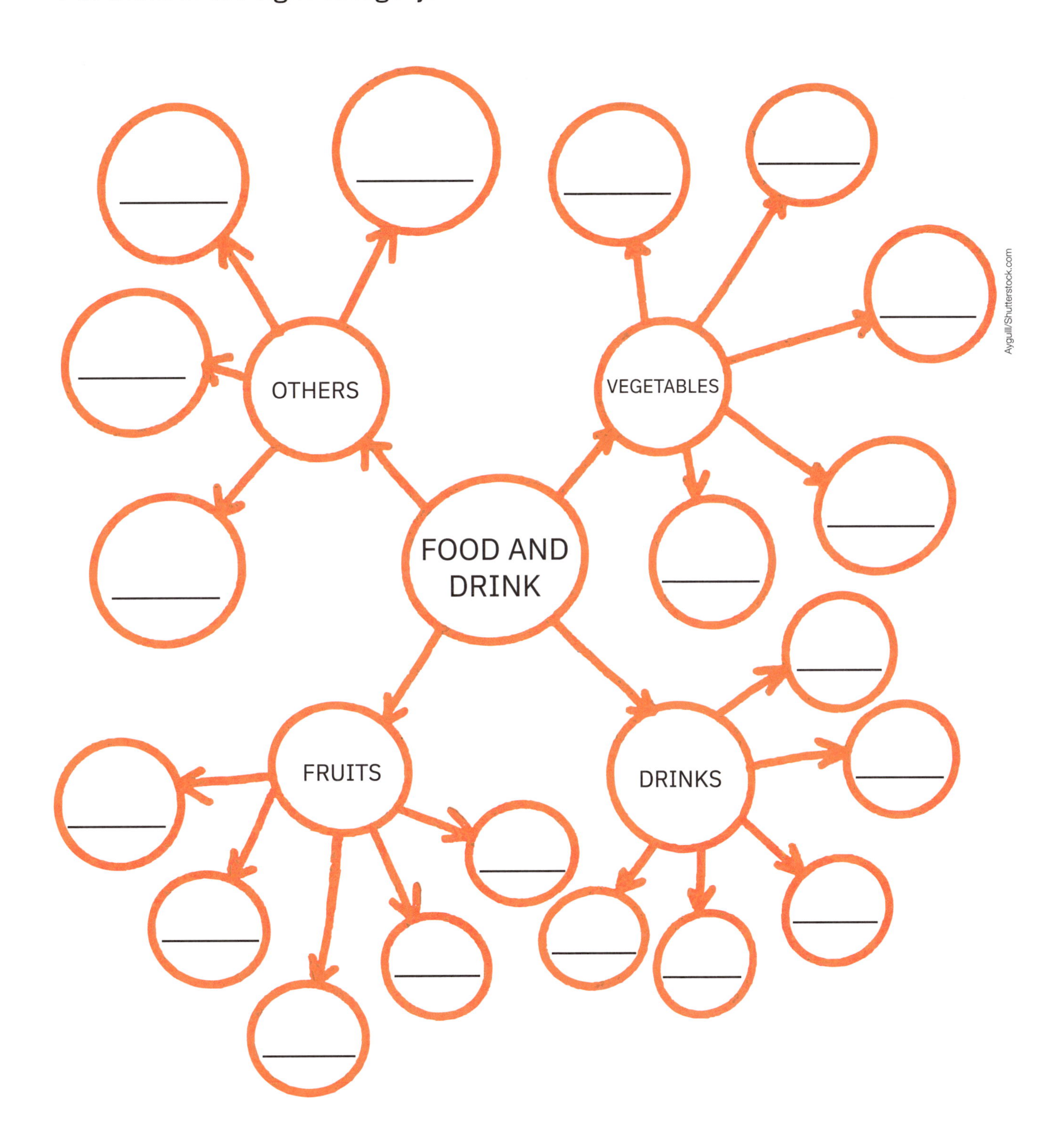

UNIT

6 A VISIT TO STEPHANY'S HOUSE

1 What part of the house is it?

bedroom • bathroom • kitchen • hall • living room
dining room • basement • attic • laundry room • garage

a) ____________________

b) ____________________

c) ____________________

d) ____________________

e) ____________________

f) ____________________

Ilustrações: Carolina Sartório

g) ____________________

h) ____________________

i) ____________________

j) ____________________

2 Find ten house rooms in the word search.

A	H	A	L	L	T	M	P	Q	C	F	D	A	J	T
P	N	W	Y	O	Y	U	Y	D	T	P	O	T	U	G
S	S	B	E	D	R	O	O	M	T	J	M	T	J	A
K	T	A	K	H	C	A	L	Q	X	Z	C	I	S	R
I	Q	S	C	I	I	K	S	X	V	H	B	C	A	A
T	A	E	P	A	J	L	P	G	Y	U	P	A	O	G
C	H	M	K	B	A	T	H	R	O	O	M	H	D	E
H	X	E	V	P	G	F	K	D	L	V	P	T	R	W
E	R	N	F	D	I	N	I	N	G	*	R	O	O	M
N	E	T	T	F	K	L	V	A	J	L	P	G	Y	O
H	D	N	H	W	Q	L	C	S	T	Y	*	X	M	S
R	L	A	U	N	D	R	Y	*	R	O	O	M	T	X
P	Q	E	X	J	G	Z	P	T	L	Z	V	Q	R	P
Z	G	Q	L	I	V	I	N	G	*	R	O	O	M	X

3 Write about your house or apartment.

UNIT

7 THE BODY

1 What body part is this? Name it.

head ✹ belly ✹ leg ✹ foot
shoulder ✹ arm ✹ hand

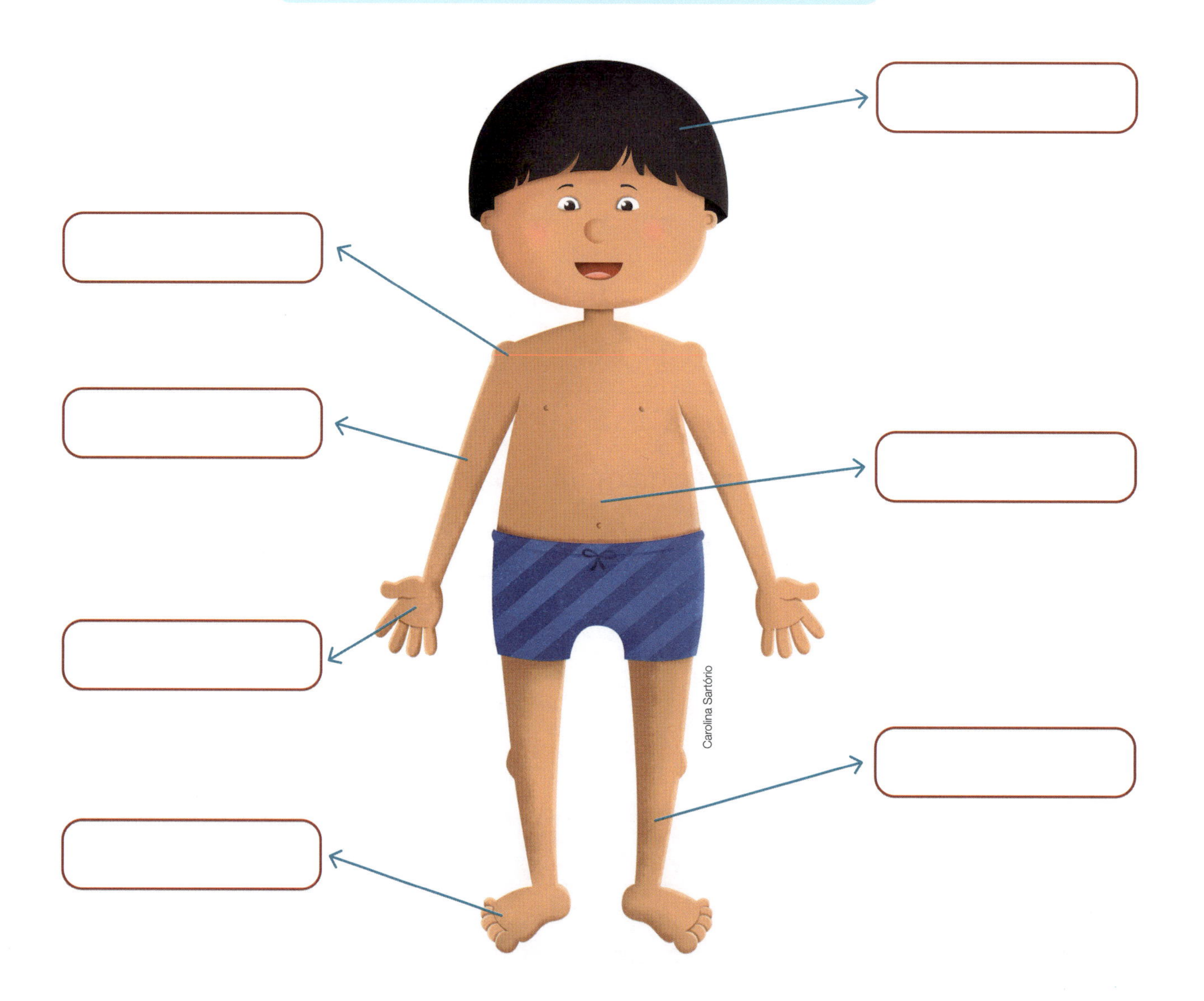

2 What is it?

hair ✷ eye ✷ nose ✷ ear ✷ mouth

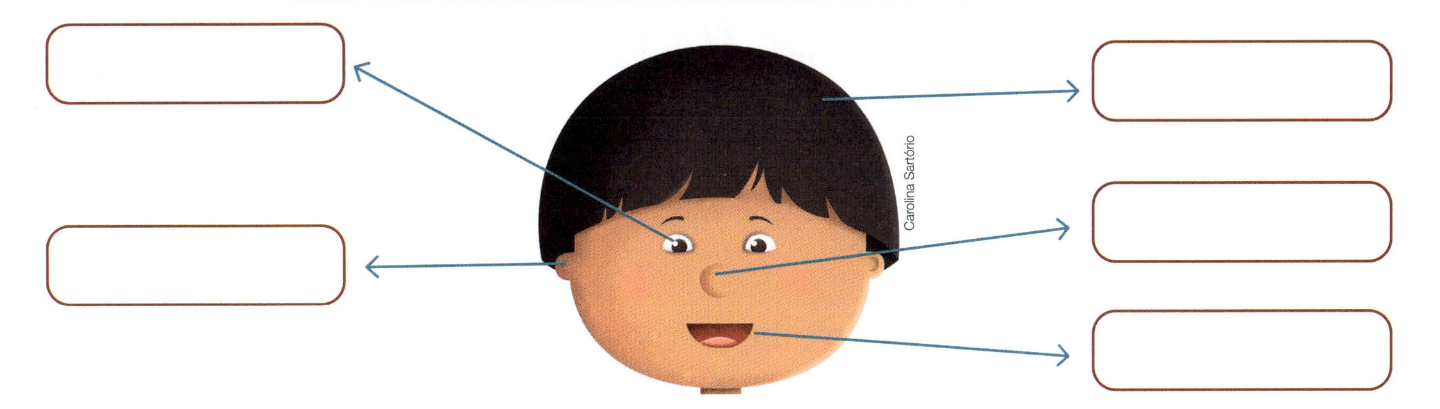

3 Find the name of nine body parts in the word search.

D	N	H	W	Q	L	C	S	T	Y	K	L	V	A	J	L	P	G
P	N	O	S	E	T	F	K	L	V	A	J	T	Y	U	I	O	U
B	P	G	F	K	D	L	L	V	A	J	L	P	G	Y	U	T	U
A	G	T	B	M	O	U	T	H	K	H	C	H	L	Q	X	Z	F
P	N	W	Y	O	Y	U	Y	D	T	P	O	U	V	X	Z	A	F
Q	E	X	J	G	Z	P	T	L	Z	V	Q	Y	U	I	O	P	A
J	H	E	A	D	E	Q	R	S	T	U	B	E	L	L	Y	S	H
C	D	Q	E	X	J	G	Z	J	G	Z	P	T	L	Z	K	L	Z
O	S	E	Q	R	Q	W	E	R	H	A	N	D	E	F	G	H	I
A	E	Y	E	S	E	F	G	X	C	V	B	N	U	Q	R	S	T
B	C	D	Q	E	X	J	G	Z	P	T	L	Z	V	T	X	V	L
T	U	V	X	Z	G	H	J	F	O	O	T	H	M	O	A	T	H
D	F	E	A	R	D	D	N	H	W	Q	L	C	S	T	Y	P	Q
E	R	N	F	D	I	N	I	S	T	U	B	S	E	F	G	H	I
E	Q	R	S	T	U	V	E	S	H	O	U	L	D	E	R	I	O

UNIT

THE MASQUERADE

1 Complete the invitation to the masquerade ball.

On August 16th
At 6 o'clock
At St. Cecil's School
Wear masks and costumes
Some juice or soda and snacks

Masquerade ball

When: ______________________

Where: ______________________

What time: ______________________

Dress code: ______________________

Bring: ______________________

Carolina Sartório

2 Match the question words to their meanings.

a) What | Place

b) Where | Time

c) When | Thing, event

3 Use **what**, **where** or **when** to complete the questions below.

a) ______________________ are you from?

I am from Brazil.

b) ______________________ is your name?

My name is George.

c) ______________________ is Copacabana?

Copacabana is located in Rio de Janeiro.

d) ______________________ is your birthday?

My birthday is in December.

e) ______________________ is your favorite food?

My favorite food is spaghetti.

f) ______________________ costume do you want to wear?

I would like to wear the butterfly costume!

g) ______________________ is the Halloween Masquerade ball?

It's in October.

h) ______________________ did you put my pirate costume?

I put it in the washing machine.

4 Match the questions with the appropriate answers.

a) Where are you from?	☐ It is Spider Man.
b) What is your favorite movie?	☐ It is in December.
c) When is your mother's birthday?	☐ It is cheeseburger.
d) When is Christmas?	☐ I am from England.
e) What is your favorite sandwich?	☐ It is on October 22nd.

5 What costume is it? Name it correctly.

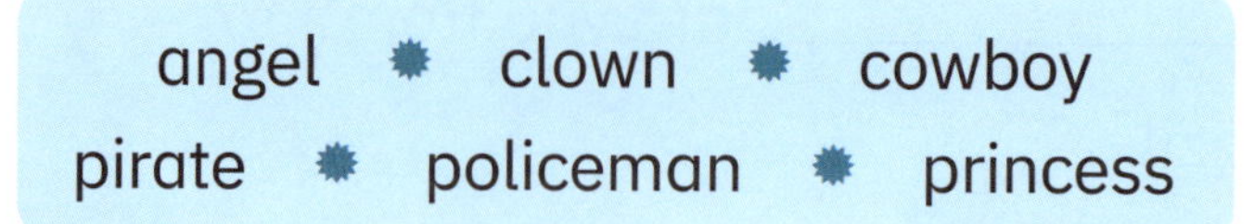

a)

____

b)

____

c)

____

d)

Ilustrações: Carolina Sartório

____

e)

____

f)

____

6 Read the card and answer the questions.

Gisell GC/Pixabay.com

a) Who is the card from?

____

b) Who is the card to?

____

c) What kind of party is it?

☐ Wedding ☐ Birthday ☐ Farewell

d) When is the party going to happen?

____

e) At what time is the party?

____

f) Where is the party?

____

7 In groups, look at the poster below about a Science Fair. Then, think about another cool school event and create a poster to let everybody know about it! Include:

- Name of the school
- Name of the event
- Date and location

Slow Area/Shutterstock.com